The Too Much Love Story

a fable in paint by priscilla hayes

The Too Much Love Story
Published in 2010 by:
Three Bean Press, LLC
P.O. Box 301711
Jamaica Plain, MA 02130
orders@threebeanpress.com • www.threebeanpress.com

Publishers Cataloging-in-Publication Data
Hayes, Priscilla
The Too Much Love Story / illustrations and text by Priscilla Hayes.
p. cm.
Summary: One family's love begins to take over a town, so they decide a baby will help solve the problem.
ISBN 978-0-9767276-4-4
[1. Children—Fiction. 2. Love—Fiction. 3. Babies—Fiction. 4. Adoption—Fiction. 5. Family—Fiction.] I. Hayes, Priscilla, Ill. II. Title.
LCCN 2010931432

Printed in Singapore

Visit www.priscillahayes.com for more information about the author and artist.

This book is dedicated to all children:

Be true to yourself,
be kind to others,
and follow your dreams.

Love,
Priscilla Hayes

Once upon a time a man and a woman lived in a house in a village by the sea.

They were a small family.

During the day they went to work, and on the weekends they enjoyed their house by the beach. But they had a problem.

They had too much love!

One day the love
started to spill out
of the windows,
out the doors
and into the
yard.

The woman decided that if they got a kitten that would solve the problem.

So they brought home a little gray kitty, and for a while it was better.

But soon it started happening again. This time the love spilled out of the windows, out the doors, into the yard and into the street.

So they went out and got a little brown puppy, and for a while it was better.

But it wasn't long before the love really started to get in the way. It spilled out

of the windows, out the doors, into the yard, onto the street, through the village and all the way to the beach.

 The people couldn't get to the movie theater to buy their tickets.

The people couldn't get to the
ice cream stand to buy their cones.

The people couldn't get to the beach to spread out their towels, play in the sand and swim in the sea.

The love got in the way so much that the children in the village couldn't even get to the park to play on the jungle gym, swing on the swings or slide down the slide.

"Whatever shall we do?" thought the man and the woman.

So they made a special plan and they waited.

As a matter of fact, the whole village waited.

Then, one day, they brought home a beautiful little baby.

The man and the woman were very happy.

As a matter of fact, the whole village was happy. Now all that extra love finally had a place to go.

Once again the people could go to the beach, spread out their towels, play in the sand, swim in the sea and buy their ice cream cones and drinks.

Once again the children could go to the park and play on the jungle gym, slide down the slide and swing on the swings.

At last the people could buy their theater tickets and go to the movies.

Now, when the family walks downtown, people say, "What a happy family. They have

just the right amount **of love**."

Everyone is very happy, especially the mommy, the daddy, the baby, the puppy and the kitty. What a wonderful family they have.